PIANO/VOCAL SELECTIONS

MILLION DOLLAR QUARTET

OPENING NIGHT: APRIL 11, 2010

⸕N⸔ NEDERLANDER THEATRE

UNDER THE DIRECTION OF
JAMES M. NEDERLANDER AND JAMES L. NEDERLANDER

RELEVANT THEATRICALS, JOHN COSSETTE PRODUCTIONS, AMERICAN POP ANTHOLOGY,
BROADWAY ACROSS AMERICA AND JAMES L. NEDERLANDER

PRESENT

MILLION D🎤LLAR QUARTET

BOOK BY COLIN ESCOTT & FLOYD MUTRUX

ORIGINAL CONCEPT AND DIRECTION BY FLOYD MUTRUX

INSPIRED BY
ELVIS PRESLEY, JOHNNY CASH, JERRY LEE LEWIS AND CARL PERKINS

FEATURING
EDDIE CLENDENING   LANCE GUEST   LEVI KREIS   ROBERT BRITTON LYONS

WITH
ELIZABETH STANLEY

AND
HUNTER FOSTER

SCENIC DESIGN	COSTUME DESIGN	LIGHTING DESIGN	SOUND DESIGN
DEREK McLANE	JANE GREENWOOD	HOWELL BINKLEY	KAI HARADA

HAIR AND WIG DESIGN	ASSOCIATE MUSIC SUPERVISOR	CASTING
TOM WATSON	AUGUST ERIKSMOEN	TELSEY + COMPANY

MARKETING DIRECTOR	PRESS REPRESENTATION	MARKETING
CAROL CHIAVETTA	BONEAU/BRYAN-BROWN	ALLIED LIVE, LLC

PRODUCTION STAGE MANAGER	PRODUCTION MANAGER	GENERAL MANAGEMENT
ROBERT WITHEROW	JUNIPER STREET PRODUCTIONS	ALAN WASSER · ALLAN WILLIAMS

MUSICAL ARRANGEMENTS AND SUPERVISION
CHUCK MEAD

DIRECTED BY
ERIC SCHAEFFER

DEVELOPED AND PRODUCED AT VILLAGE THEATRE, ISSAQUAH, WASHINGTON
ROBB HUNT, PRODUCER · STEVE TOMKINS, ARTISTIC DIRECTOR

ORIGINALLY PRESENTED BY SEASIDE MUSIC THEATER
TIPPIN DAVIDSON, PRODUCER
LESTER MALIZIA, ARTISTIC DIRECTOR

ISBN 978-1-61780-693-3

HAL•LEONARD® CORPORATION

7777 W. BLUEMOUND RD. P.O. BOX 13819 MILWAUKEE, WI 53213

Visit Hal Leonard Online at
www.halleonard.com

4   **BLUE SUEDE SHOES**

7   **REAL WILD CHILD**

10   **MATCHBOX**

15   **WHO DO YOU LOVE**

19   **FOLSOM PRISON BLUES**

21   **FEVER**

24   **MEMORIES ARE MADE OF THIS**

29   **THAT'S ALL RIGHT**

31   **BROWN-EYED HANDSOME MAN**

35   **DOWN BY THE RIVERSIDE**

40   **SIXTEEN TONS**

42   **MY BABE**

45   **LONG TALL SALLY**

48   **THERE WILL BE PEACE IN THE VALLEY FOR ME**

51   **I WALK THE LINE**

53   **I HEAR YOU KNOCKING**

56   **PARTY ((LET'S HAVE A) PARTY)**

58   **GREAT BALLS OF FIRE**

62   **HOUND DOG**

65   **(GHOST) RIDERS IN THE SKY**

73   **SEE YOU LATER, ALLIGATOR**

76   **WHOLE LOTTA SHAKIN' GOIN' ON**

BLUE SUEDE SHOES

Words and Music by
CARL LEE PERKINS

Brightly, not too fast

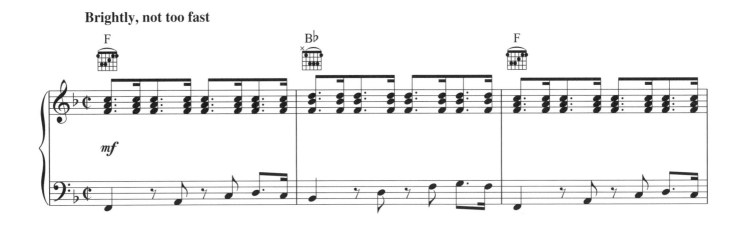

Well, it's one for the mon-ey, two for the show,

three to get read-y, now go, cat, go! But don't you

REAL WILD CHILD

Words and Music by JOHNNY O'KEEFE,
JOHNNY GREENAN and DAVE OWENS

break loose, gon - na keep a-mov-in' wild, gon-na keep a-swing-in', ba-by, I'm a

real wild child. { Gon - na meet all my friends, gon - na have my-self a ball. Gon - na
Not a doubt, not a may - be, I'm a real wild child. Don't-cha

tell my friends, gon - na tell them all that I'm a
pout, my ba - by, when I start a - run - nin' wild, 'cause I'm a

wild one, }
wild one, }   ooh yay: I'm a wild one.

Gon - na break loose, gon - na keep a - mov - in' wild, gon - na

keep a - swing - in', ba - by, I'm a real wild child.

Well, I'm a

Repeat and Fade

MATCHBOX

Words and Music by
CARL LEE PERKINS

Bright Shuffle

for you, ba - by, leave me here in ___ mis - er - y. ___ *(Spoken:)* *All right!*

Well, ___ let me be ___ your lit - tle dog ___ till your big dog comes; ___

WHO DO YOU LOVE

Words and Music by
ELLAS McDANIEL

brand new chim-ney made on top, made from a hu-man

skull. Now come on, ba-by, let's take a lit-tle walk and tell me:

Play 4 times

Who do you love? ___ Ar-lene took me

by the hand, ___ she said, "Oo-ee, dad-dy, I un-der-stand.

Play 3 times

Who do you love? ___ Who do you love?" ___

___ The night was black and the night was blue ___ and a-

round the cor - ner an ice wag - on flew. A bump was hit and

some - bod - y screamed. You should have heard just what I seen. Now

Play 3 times

Who do you love? ___ Who do you love? _

___ I got a tomb - stone hand, a grave - yard mine. I

lived long e - nough and I ain't scared o' dy - in'. Who do you love? _

Play 3 times

___ Who do you love? ___

FOLSOM PRISON BLUES

Words and Music by
JOHN R. CASH

Additional Lyrics

3. I bet there's rich folks eatin' in a fancy dining car;
   They're prob'ly drinkin' coffee and smokin' big cigars.
   But I know I had it comin', I know I can't be free,
   But those people keep a-movin', and that's what tortures me.

4. Well, if they freed me from this prison, if that railroad train was mine,
   I bet I'd move on over a little farther down the line.
   Far from Folsom Prison, that's where I want to stay,
   And I'd let that lonesome whistle blow my blues away.

FEVER

Words and Music by JOHN DAVENPORT
and EDDIE COOLEY

Moderately, with a beat

1. Nev - er know how much I love you, nev - er know how much I
2. Sun lights up the day - time, moon lights up the
3. Ro - me - o loved Ju - li - et. Ju - li - et, she felt the
4. Cap - tain Smith and Po - ca - hon - tas had a ver - y mad af -
5. Now you've lis - tened to my sto - ry. Here's the point that I have

care. When you put your arms a - round me, I get a
night. I light up when you call my name, and you
same. When he put his arms a - round her, he said,
fair. When her dad - dy tried to kill him, she said,
made. Chicks were born to give you fe - ver, be it

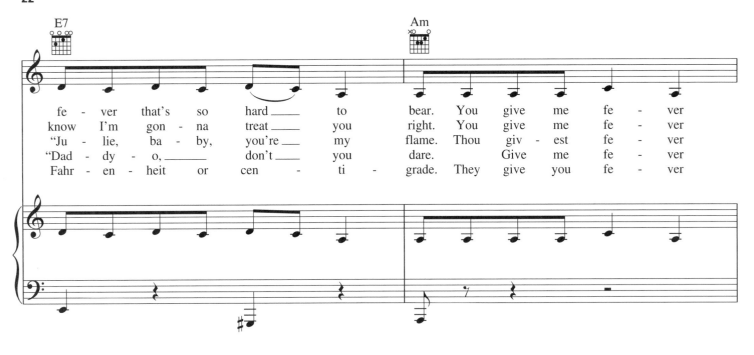

fe - ver that's so hard ___ to bear. You give me fe - ver
know I'm gon - na treat ___ you right. You give me fe - ver
"Ju - lie, ba - by, you're ___ my flame. Thou giv - est fe - ver
"Dad - dy - o, ___ don't ___ you dare. Give me fe - ver
Fahr - en - heit or cen - ti - grade. They give you fe - ver

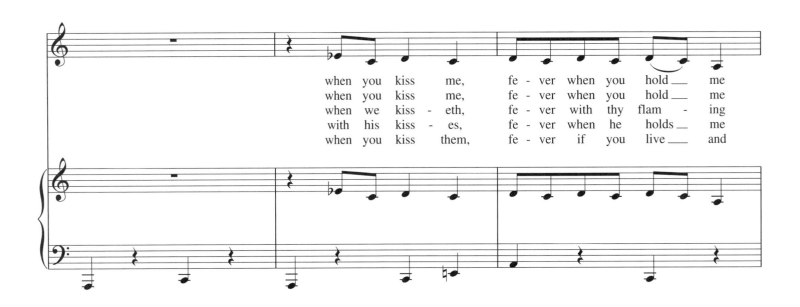

when you kiss me, fe - ver when you hold ___ me
when you kiss me, fe - ver when you hold ___ me
when we kiss - eth, fe - ver with thy flam - ing
with his kiss - es, fe - ver when he holds ___ me
when you kiss them, fe - ver if you live ___ and

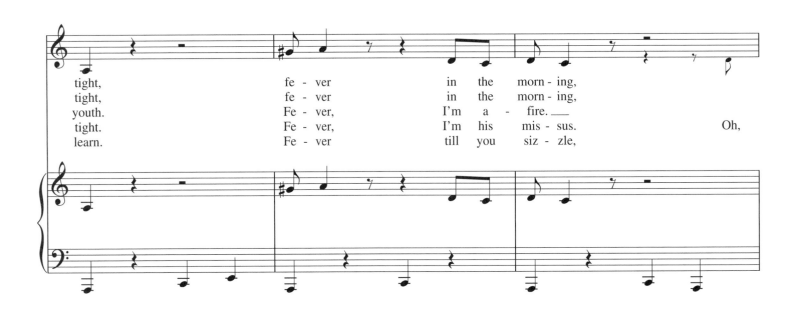

tight, fe - ver in the morn - ing,
tight, fe - ver in the morn - ing,
youth. Fe - ver, I'm a - fire. ___
tight. Fe - ver, I'm his mis - sus. Oh,
learn. Fe - ver till you siz - zle,

MEMORIES ARE MADE OF THIS

Words and Music by RICHARD DEHR,
FRANK MILLER and TERRY GILKYSON

THAT'S ALL RIGHT

Words and Music by
ARTHUR CRUDUP

Moderate Blues

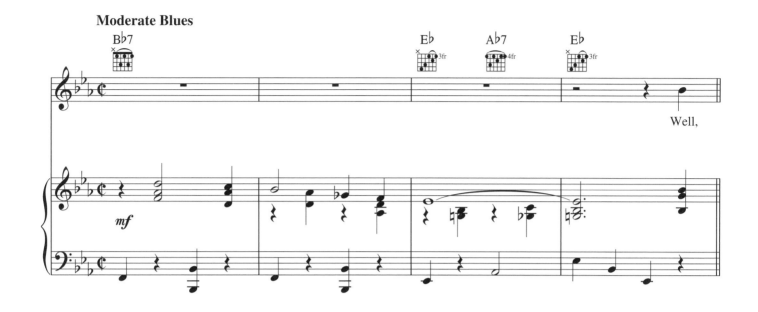

Well,

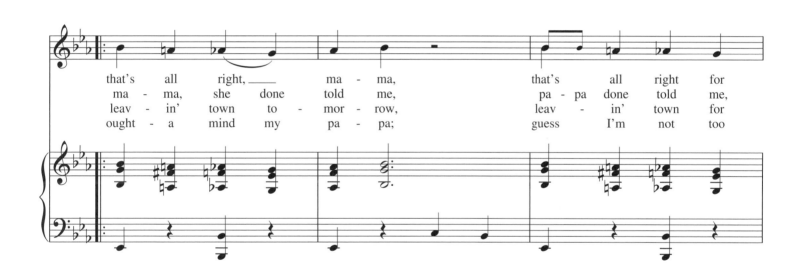

that's all right, ___ ma-ma,   that's all right for
ma-ma, she done told me,   pa-pa done told me,
leav- in' town to-mor-row,   leav- in' town for
ought- a mind my pa- pa;   guess I'm not too

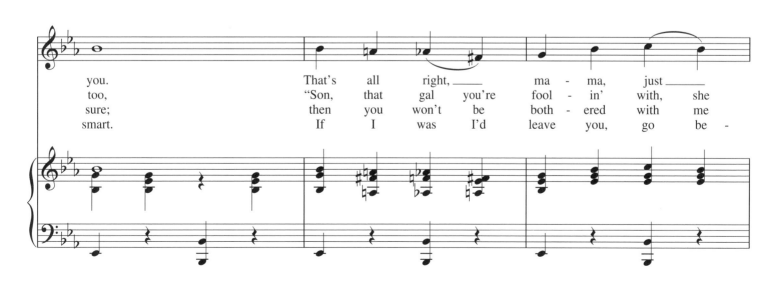

you.   That's all right, ___ ma-ma, just ___
too,   "Son, that gal you're fool- in' with, she
sure;   then you won't be both- ered with me
smart.   If I was I'd leave you, go be -

BROWN-EYED HANDSOME MAN

Words and Music by
CHUCK BERRY

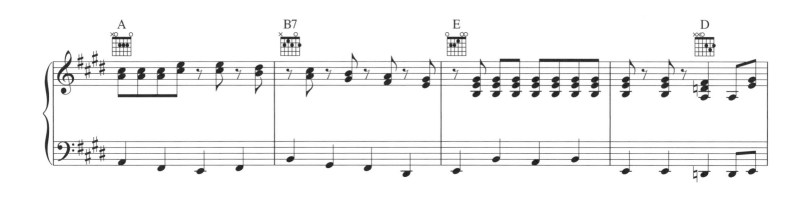

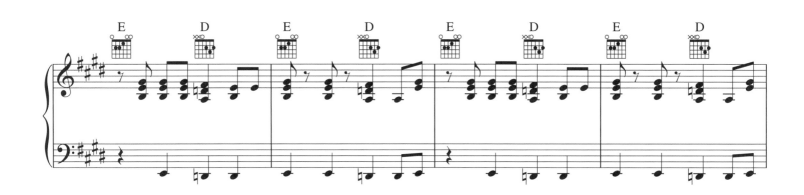

Well, the

DOWN BY THE RIVERSIDE

African American Spiritual

SIXTEEN TONS

Words and Music by
MERLE TRAVIS

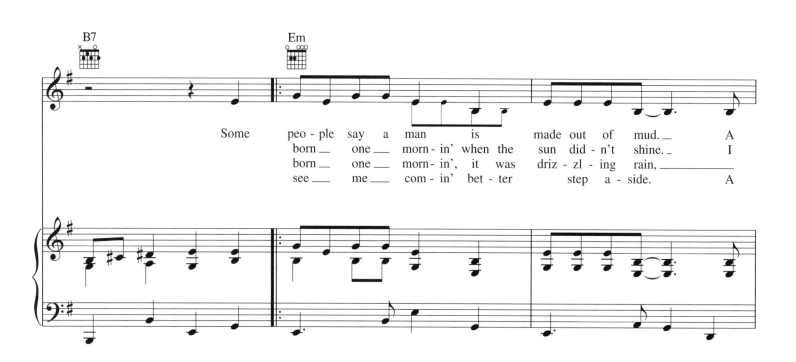

Some peo-ple say a man is made out of mud. A
born _ one _ morn-in' when the sun did-n't shine. _ I
born _ one _ morn-in', it was driz-zl-ing rain, _____ I
see _ me _ com-in' bet-ter step a - side. A

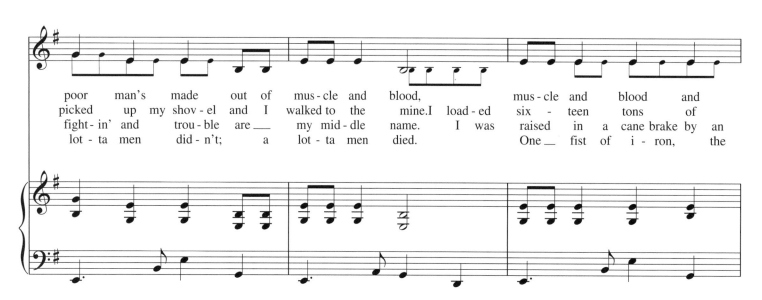

poor man's made out of mus-cle and blood, mus-cle and blood and
picked up my shov-el and I walked to the mine. I load-ed six - teen tons of
fight-in' and trou-ble are _ my mid-dle name. I was raised in a cane brake by an
lot-ta men did-n't; a lot-ta men died. One _ fist of i-ron, the

MY BABE

Written by WILLIE DIXON

LONG TALL SALLY

Words and Music by ENOTRIS JOHNSON,
RICHARD PENNIMAN and ROBERT BLACKWELL

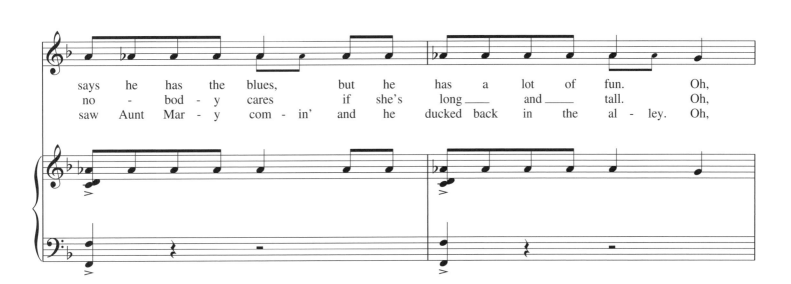

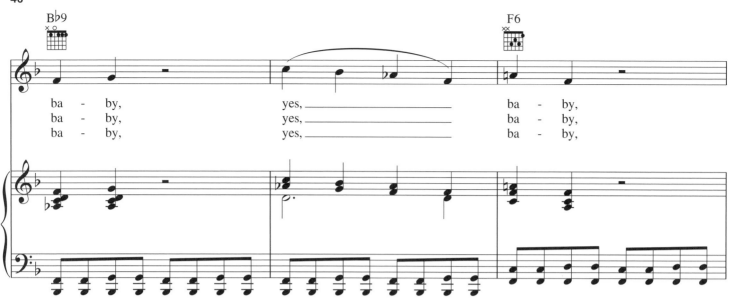

ba - by,   yes, _____ ba - by,
ba - by,   yes, _____ ba - by,
ba - by,   yes, _____ ba - by,

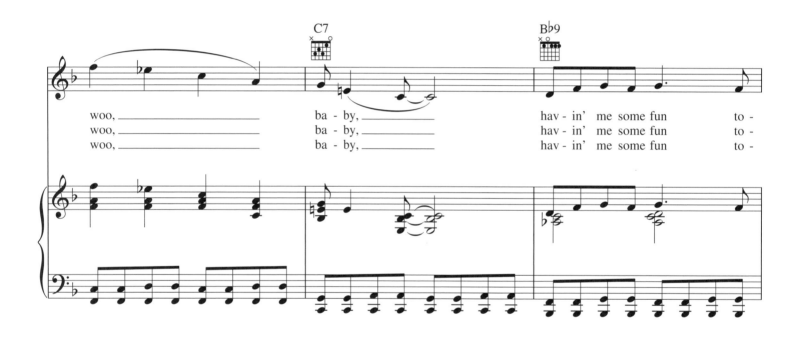

woo, _____ ba - by, _____ hav - in' me some fun   to -
woo, _____ ba - by, _____ hav - in' me some fun   to -
woo, _____ ba - by, _____ hav - in' me some fun   to -

night. _____   Yeah! _____   Well,
night. _____   Well, I
night. _____   Yeah! _____   We're gon - na

THERE WILL BE PEACE IN THE VALLEY FOR ME

Words and Music by
THOMAS A. DORSEY

me. I pray no more sor - row and sad - ness or

trou - ble will be, there'll be peace ___ in the val - ley for

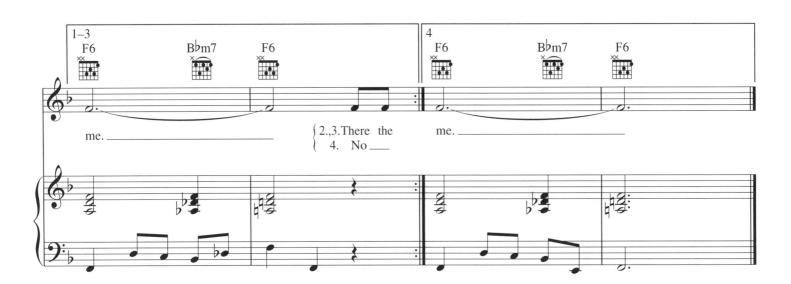

1–3
me. ___ 2.,3.There the me. ___
4. No ___

4
me. ___

Additional Lyrics

4. No headaches or heartaches or misunderstands,
No, confusion or trouble won't be.
No frowns to defile, just a big endless smile,
There'll be peace and contentment for me.
Chorus

I WALK THE LINE

Words and Music by
JOHN R. CASH

Additional Lyrics

3. As sure as night is dark and day is light,
   I keep you on my mind both day and night.
   And happiness I've known proves that it's right.
   Because you're mine I walk the line.

4. You've got a way to keep me on your side.
   You give me cause for love that I can't hide.
   For you I know I'd even try to turn the tide.
   Because you're mine I walk the line.

5. I keep a close watch on this heart of mine.
   I keep my eyes wide open all the time.
   I keep the ends out for the tie that binds.
   Because you're mine I walk the line.

I HEAR YOU KNOCKING

Words and Music by DAVE BARTHOLOMEW
and PEARL KING

PARTY
((Let's Have A) Party)

Words and Music by
JESSIE MAE ROBINSON

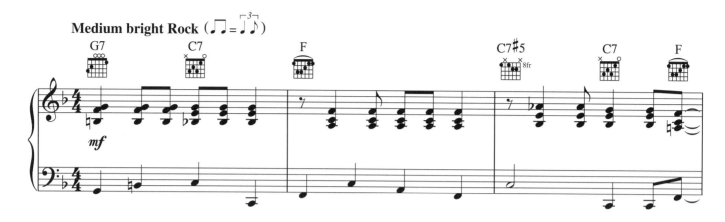

Medium bright Rock

I feel it in my leg; I feel it in my shoe.
peo-ple like to rock; some peo-ple like to roll. But
nev-er kissed a bear; I've nev-er kissed a goon. But
Honk-y Tonk-y Joe is knock-in' at the door.

Tell me, pur-ty ba-by, if you think you feel it, too.
mov-in' and a groov-in' gon-na sat-is-fy my soul.
I can shake a chick-en in the mid-dle of the room. } Let's have a
Bring him in and fill him up and set him on the floor.

GREAT BALLS OF FIRE

Words and Music by OTIS BLACKWELL
and JACK HAMMER

Bright Rock

You shake my nerves and you rat-tle my brain. _
Instrumental

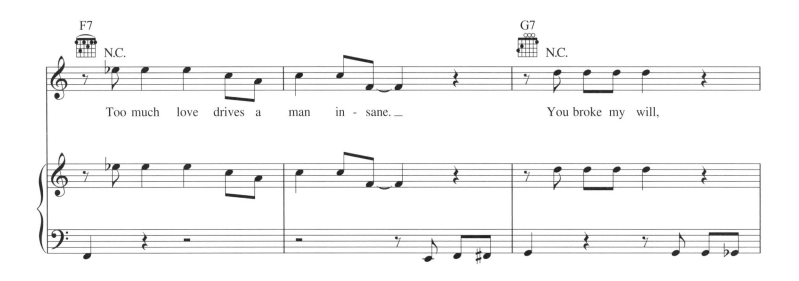

Too much love drives a man in-sane. _ You broke my will,

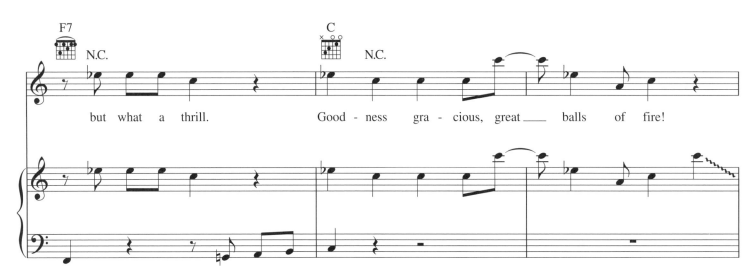

but what a thrill. Good-ness gra-cious, great __ balls of fire!

HOUND DOG

Words and Music by JERRY LEIBER
and MIKE STOLLER

Moderate Shuffle

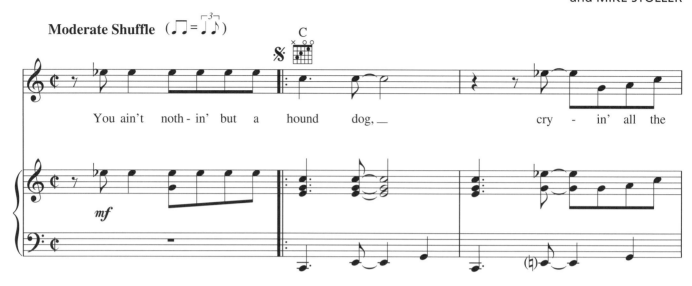

You ain't noth-in' but a hound dog, ___ cry-in' all the

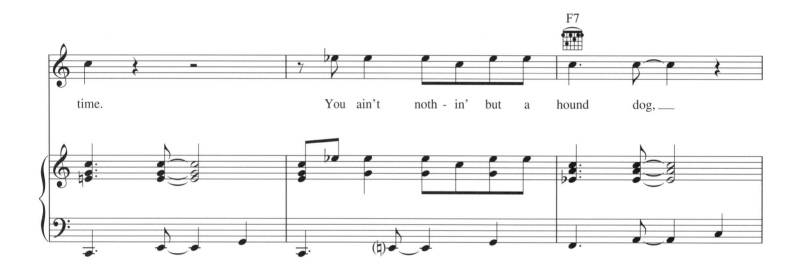

time. You ain't noth-in' but a hound dog, ___

cry-in' all the time. Well, ___ you ain't

To Coda

(GHOST) RIDERS IN THE SKY
(A Cowboy Legend)

By STAN JONES

Driving and mysterious ♩ = 116 - 120

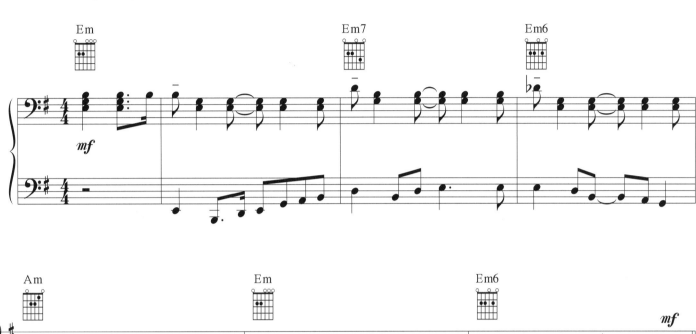

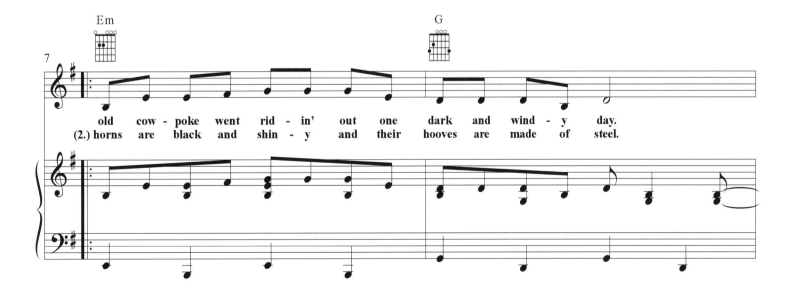

old cow - poke went rid - in' out one dark and wind - y day.
(2.) horns are black and shin - y and their hooves are made of steel.

SEE YOU LATER, ALLIGATOR

Words and Music by
ROBERT GUIDRY

with an - oth - er man to - day. __ When I asked her what's the
near - ly made me lose my head. __ But the next time that I
you know my love is just for you. __ Won't you say that you'll for -
I know you meant it just for play." _ Don't you know you real - ly

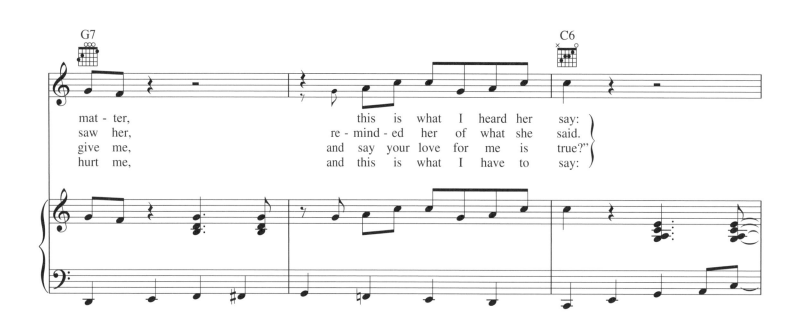

mat - ter, this is what I heard her say:
saw her, re - mind - ed her of what she said.
give me, and say your love for me is true?"
hurt me, and this is what I have to say:

"See you lat - er, al - li - ga - tor, af - ter 'while, __ croc - o -

WHOLE LOTTA SHAKIN' GOIN' ON

Words and Music by
DAVID WILLIAMS

Moderately, with a solid beat

Come on o - ver, ba - by, whole lot - ta shak - in' goin' on, ___

come on o - ver, ba - by, an' ba - by you can't go wrong, ___

ain't no-bod - y fak - in', whole lot - ta shak - in' goin' on. ___